RANJOT SINGH CHAHAL

# How to Know Your Powers

*A Perfect Guide to Personal Growth and Success*



Rana Books

*First published by Rana Books ( UK , INDIA )  2023*



*First edition*

# Contents

# I

# Part One

# 1

# Understanding Abilities: An Overview

The concept of abilities refers to the skills talents or qualities that an individual possesses which enable them to perform certain tasks or achieve specific outcomes. Abilities are inherent in individuals and can be developed and enhanced through learning and experience. They play a crucial role in determining an individual's success and performance in various areas of life including education career personal relationships and overall well-being.

Different Types of Abilities:

Abilities can be broadly categorized into various types based on their nature and the areas of life they impact. Some of the key types of abilities include:

1. Cognitive Abilities: Cognitive abilities are mental skills that are crucial for processing analyzing and interpreting information. These abilities include problem-solving critical thinking logical reasoning memory attention and decision-

making. Cognitive abilities are essential for academic success professional growth and effective functioning in everyday life.

For example someone with strong cognitive abilities may excel in subjects such as mathematics science or any discipline that requires analytical thinking. They can quickly grasp complex concepts analyze data and make sound judgments.

2. Physical Abilities: Physical abilities refer to an individual's physical attributes and skills. These include strength endurance flexibility agility coordination and sensory perception. Physical abilities play a vital role in various physical activities sports and occupations that require physical exertion.

For instance a professional athlete requires exceptional physical abilities to excel in their sport. A gymnast needs flexibility and balance while a sprinter relies on speed and explosive power.

3. Social and Emotional Abilities: Social and emotional abilities involve the capacity to understand manage and express emotions effectively and navigate social interactions. These abilities include empathy self-awareness emotional intelligence communication skills conflict resolution leadership and teamwork.

For example individuals with strong social and emotional abilities can build and maintain healthy relationships resolve conflicts peacefully and effectively collaborate with others. They are also more adept at managing stress and adapting to challenging situations.

4. Communication Abilities: Communication abilities encom-

pass the skills required to convey information ideas and emotions effectively. These include verbal communication non-verbal communication active listening public speaking writing and persuasion skills.

Effective communication abilities are vital in personal and professional contexts. They enable individuals to express their thoughts clearly persuade others build rapport and resolve conflicts. A skilled communicator can engage an audience deliver compelling presentations and influence others positively.

5. Creative Abilities: Creative abilities refer to the capacity to think and generate innovative ideas concepts and solutions. These include creative thinking imagination problem-solving artistic skills and the ability to see possibilities beyond conventional boundaries.

Creative abilities are highly valued in fields such as art design writing innovation and entrepreneurship. An individual with exceptional creative abilities can think outside the box come up with unique solutions and add value through their imaginative ideas.

Identifying Your Unique Abilities:

Identifying your unique abilities is essential for personal and professional growth. Recognizing and leveraging your strengths can help you make informed decisions about career choices guide your personal development and maximize your potential. Here are some steps to identify your unique abilities:

1. Self-Reflection: Take time to reflect on yourself your experiences and your past achievements. Consider activities tasks or situations where you felt confident competent and passionate. Identify the skills and qualities that contributed to your success and satisfaction in those instances.

For example if you consistently excel at organizing events and managing logistics it indicates your ability to plan coordinate and multitask effectively.

2. Feedback from Others: Seek feedback from trusted individuals in your personal and professional circles. Ask them about your strengths areas where they perceive you as exceptionally skilled or talented and how they perceive your abilities.

Others may have insights and observations about you that you may not have considered. Their perspectives can help validate your own self-assessment and highlight strengths you may have overlooked.

3. Assessments and Surveys: Consider taking ability-focused assessments or surveys designed to identify and evaluate specific abilities. Many online platforms offer tests and questionnaires that can help you gain insights into your cognitive emotional or other abilities.

These assessments can provide objective data and insights into areas where you excel naturally allowing you to further develop and leverage those abilities.

4. Trial and Exploration: Engage in diverse activities projects

and opportunities to explore different areas and gauge your level of interest and prowess. Trying out new endeavors can help you discover hidden abilities that you may not have previously recognized.

For instance joining a public speaking club or taking up a painting class might uncover communication or artistic abilities that you were unaware of.

5. Seek Expert Guidance: If you find it challenging to identify or understand your unique abilities consider seeking the guidance of professionals such as career counselors or coaches. They can help you explore your potential and provide valuable insights and strategies for leveraging your abilities effectively.

Remember identifying your unique abilities is an ongoing process influenced by your personal growth experiences and changing circumstances. As you progress in your personal and professional journey continue to reassess and refine your understanding of your abilities to maximize your potential and achieve success.

Conclusion:

Understanding and harnessing your abilities is essential for personal fulfillment professional growth and overall well-being. Abilities come in various forms and can be developed through learning and experience. By identifying your unique abilities you can make informed decisions about career paths personal development and realize your full potential. Engaging in self-reflection seeking feedback using assessments exploring new activities and seeking expert guidance are all ways to identify and leverage your abilities effectively. So take the time to explore and understand your unique abilities and embrace the opportunities they present for personal and professional success.

# 2

# Exploripng the Power Within: Self-Discovery

Self-discovery is a lifelong journey of exploring and understanding the depths of who we are as individuals. It encompasses various aspects such as self-awareness personal growth assessing strengths and weaknesses and uncovering passions and interests. The process of self-discovery allows us to tap into the power within us unlocking our true potential and leading to a more fulfilling and purpose-driven life. In this Chapter we will delve deeply into these concepts providing explanations and examples to help you embark on your own journey of self-discovery.

I. Self-Awareness and Personal Growth:

Self-awareness is the foundation of self-discovery. It involves developing a deep understanding of one's thoughts emotions values beliefs strengths weaknesses and motivations. It allows us to gain insights into our own behavior and reactions identify patterns and make conscious choices aligned with our true selves.

Example: Let's consider an individual who struggles with managing anger. Through self-awareness they become aware that their anger stems from feelings of injustice and a need for control. By recognizing these triggers they can begin to respond to situations in a more constructive and controlled manner leading to personal growth.

Personal growth encompasses the continuous development and improvement of oneself. It involves setting goals seeking new experiences acquiring new skills and challenging oneself to expand beyond comfort zones. Personal growth is essential for self-discovery as it allows us to evolve learn from setbacks and align our actions with our values and aspirations.

Example: An individual who wishes to enhance their communication skills may embark on a personal growth journey by attending workshops reading books and practicing active listening techniques. Through this self-improvement process they gain valuable insights into their communication style and become more effective in their interactions.

II. Assessing Your Strengths and Weaknesses:

Assessing strengths and weaknesses is a crucial step in self-discovery. It involves identifying and understanding our abilities talents and areas for improvement. By acknowledging and leveraging our strengths we can enhance our confidence and pursue areas that align with our natural aptitudes. Conversely recognizing weaknesses allows us to address them develop new skills or seek help when necessary.

Example: An individual passionate about leadership may

identify strengths such as excellent communication problem-solving and strategic thinking skills. With this self-awareness they can pursue leadership positions or engage in activities that further develop their leadership abilities. At the same time they may recognize a weakness in public speaking prompting them to seek opportunities to improve this skill.

III. Uncovering Your Passions and Interests:

Exploring and uncovering our passions and interests is an integral part of self-discovery. Passions are activities or causes that ignite a deep sense of excitement purpose and fulfillment within us. Interests on the other hand are areas of curiosity and enjoyment that engage our attention and motivate us to learn and grow.

Example: Imagine an individual who finds immense joy in painting. They lose track of time as they immerse themselves in creating art experiencing a profound sense of fulfillment. By recognizing this passion they can dedicate more time and effort to cultivate their artistic abilities leading to a greater sense of purpose and happiness.

Uncovering our passions and interests often involves experimentation exploration and reflection. It requires us to step out of our comfort zones and try new activities allowing us to discover what truly resonates with our authentic selves.

Example: Someone curious about travel might engage in various forms of exploration such as backpacking road trips or even international volunteering. Through these experiences they may realize a deep passion for cultural immersion and subsequently pursue a career in international relations or become a travel writer.

Conclusion:

Self-discovery is a continuous and transformative journey that empowers us to tap into our inner potential leading to personal growth and fulfillment. By nurturing self-awareness identifying our strengths and weaknesses and uncovering our passions and interests we can align our actions and choices with our authentic selves. Remember self-discovery is a deeply personal process and it may take time and effort to fully explore and understand our true nature. Embrace the journey be open to self-reflection and seize the power within to create a life of purpose joy and self-fulfillment.

# 3

# Nurturing Your Mental Abilities

In today's fast-paced and information-driven world nurturing and enhancing our mental abilities has become crucial. Whether you're a student professional or simply striving for personal growth developing cognitive skills enhancing critical thinking and strengthening memory and concentration can significantly improve your overall mental performance. In this essay we will explore these three aspects of nurturing your mental abilities providing examples and techniques to help you effectively cultivate these skills.

1. Developing Cognitive Skills:

Cognitive skills refer to mental processes that enable us to acquire process understand and analyze information. Developing these skills can improve your learning ability problem-solving skills and overall cognitive functions. Here are some effective ways to foster cognitive skills:

a. Reading and Engaging with Diverse Materials:

Reading regularly exposes your mind to new ideas concepts and perspectives. It stimulates critical thinking expands vocabulary and enhances analytical skills. Engaging with diverse materials such as books Chapters and research papers allows you to explore various subjects and domains broadening your knowledge base.

For example instead of sticking to one genre try reading books from different genres like fiction non-fiction science philosophy and history. This will challenge your mind to adapt to different writing styles and subject matters improving your cognitive flexibility.

b. Engaging in Problem-Solving Activities:

Actively engaging in problem-solving activities enhances cognitive skills such as logical reasoning analytical thinking and creativity. Puzzles riddles brain teasers and strategy games like chess and Sudoku are excellent exercises to develop cognitive abilities.

For instance solving puzzles like crosswords or playing strategy games forces your brain to think critically make connections and strategize. Over time these activities improve your problem-solving skills memory and attention to detail.

c. Learning a New Skill:

Learning a new skill not only enhances your abilities in that particular area but also develops cognitive functions such as memory attention and coordination. Whether it's playing a musical instrument painting coding or even learning a new language the process of acquiring new knowledge and mastering a skill stimulates brain connectivity and strengthens cognitive abilities.

For example learning to play a musical instrument requires coordination between the motor skills and reading musical notes boosting memory concentration and cognitive flexibility.

2. Enhancing Critical Thinking:

Critical thinking is the ability to objectively analyze and evaluate information arguments and situations. It involves questioning assumptions considering multiple perspectives and making informed decisions. Enhancing critical thinking skills allows you to navigate complex issues identify biases and reach logical conclusions. Here are some strategies to enhance critical thinking:

a. Socratic Questioning:

Socratic questioning is a technique used to stimulate and guide critical thinking by asking thought-provoking questions. By analyzing assumptions evidence and reasoning behind a statement or argument you can develop a deeper understanding and make more informed judgments.

For example when faced with a persuasive argument you can use Socratic questioning by asking: "What evidence supports this claim?" or "What are the underlying assumptions of this statement?"

b. Exploring Multiple Perspectives:

Avoiding cognitive biases and broadening your perspective

is a crucial aspect of critical thinking. Actively seeking alternative viewpoints and considering diverse perspectives can help you critically assess information and make well-rounded judgments.

For instance when evaluating a controversial topic read Chapters or watch videos that offer different perspectives. This allows you to analyze the merits and weaknesses of each side and form a more balanced understanding.

c. Analyzing and Evaluating Information:
In a world filled with information overload developing the ability to analyze and evaluate information is essential. This involves distinguishing between reliable and biased sources assessing the credibility of claims and understanding the logical coherence of arguments.

For example when reading a news Chapter critically evaluate the sources of information look for supporting evidence and consider counterarguments before accepting it as valid and reliable.

3. Strengthening Memory and Concentration:

Memory and concentration are fundamental cognitive functions that play a vital role in daily life learning and productivity. Improving memory and concentration can enhance overall mental performance and enable you to absorb and retain information effectively. Here are some techniques to strengthen memory and concentration:

a. Practice Active Learning:

Active learning involves engaging actively with the material you are trying to learn. Instead of passive reading or listening take notes summarize information and explain concepts aloud. This requires you to actively process and retain information reinforcing memory and concentration.

For example while studying try to explain key concepts or ideas to yourself or someone else as this reinforces understanding and memory recall.

b. Regular Physical Exercise:

Physical exercise has been proven to have numerous cognitive benefits. It boosts blood flow to the brain improves concentration and enhances memory retention. Engaging in regular aerobic exercise such as jogging swimming or cycling can significantly improve cognitive function.

For instance studies have shown that individuals who engage in regular physical exercise have better memory and attention span compared to those leading sedentary lifestyles.

c. Utilize Memory Techniques:

There are various memory techniques such as mnemonics visualization and chunking that can enhance memory recall. Mnemonics involve associating information with memorable cues or creating acronyms to aid in memory retention. Visualization involves creating mental images to associate with the information making it easier to recall.

For example to remember a list of items you can create a memorable story that connects each item in a logical sequence. This technique enhances memory recall by associating information with a cohesive narrative.

In conclusion nurturing your mental abilities is crucial for personal growth academic success and professional development. Developing cognitive skills enhancing critical thinking and strengthening memory and concentration provide a foundation for effective learning problem-solving and overall mental well-being. By implementing the strategies discussed in this essay such as reading diverse materials engaging in problem-solving activities utilizing critical thinking techniques and practicing memory improvement techniques you can actively nurture and enhance your mental abilities to reach your full potential.

# 4

# Embracing Emotional Intelligence

Emotional intelligence often referred to as EQ (emotional quotient is a crucial aspect of human behavior and interaction. It involves the ability to recognize understand and manage emotions both in oneself and others. Embracing emotional intelligence is about developing self-awareness regulating emotions effectively and building strong interpersonal skills to navigate relationships and social situations.

Understanding Emotional Intelligence:

1. Self-Awareness:

Self-awareness is the foundation of emotional intelligence. It involves recognizing and understanding your own emotions strengths weaknesses values and how they influence your behavior. Being self-aware allows you to have a clearer perception of yourself and others enabling you to make informed decisions and understand emotional triggers.

For example a person with high self-awareness may recognize that they become impatient when faced with delays and can take steps to manage their impatience more effectively such as practicing patience-building exercises or employing time-management strategies.

2. Self-Regulation:

Once you are aware of your emotions the next step is regulating them effectively. Self-regulation involves managing your emotions impulses and reactions in a way that is socially acceptable and constructive. It is about avoiding impulsive behaviors and responding thoughtfully even in challenging situations.

For instance if someone receives criticism at work instead of reacting defensively or getting angry they can practice self-regulation by taking a moment to understand the feedback and respond constructively seeking ways to improve their performance.

Managing Your Emotions:

1. Emotional Awareness:

Emotional awareness is the ability to identify and understand the emotions you experience as well as the causes and consequences of those emotions. It involves recognizing the physiological changes thoughts and behaviors associated with specific emotions.

For instance if you notice your heart racing and feeling anxious before giving a presentation being emotionally aware allows you to identify these physical and emotional signs and practice techniques such as deep breathing or visualization to calm down and manage your anxiety effectively.

2. Emotional Resilience:

Emotional resilience refers to the ability to bounce back from setbacks challenges and adversity. It is about staying strong and maintaining a positive outlook even in difficult circumstances. Emotional resilience enables individuals to navigate stress setbacks and obstacles with greater ease and adaptability.

For example a resilient person may face a rejection in a job interview without becoming disheartened. Instead they see it as an opportunity to learn and grow and they continue to apply to other suitable positions with enthusiasm and persistence.

Building Empathy and Interpersonal Skills:

1. Empathy:

Empathy is the ability to understand and share the emotions of others putting oneself in someone else's shoes. It involves actively listening being non-judgmental and demonstrating understanding and concern for others' emotions and experiences.

For instance if a friend shares their struggles with you displaying empathy would mean listening attentively validating their feelings and offering support and encouragement.

2. Effective Communication:

Effective communication is crucial for building strong interpersonal relationships. It involves expressing oneself clearly and openly actively listening to others and engaging in meaningful and respectful dialogue. Effective communication enables individuals to connect build trust and resolve conflicts more effectively.

For example in a team setting effective communication involves expressing oneself clearly actively listening to teammates' ideas and concerns and fostering an environment where everyone's voice is heard and respected.

3. Collaboration and Teamwork:

Collaboration and teamwork are essential skills in both personal and professional settings. They involve working together towards a common goal valuing diverse perspectives and effectively utilizing each team member's strengths. Collaboration fosters creativity innovation and productivity.

For instance in a workplace project effective collaboration requires recognizing each team member's unique expertise assigning roles and responsibilities accordingly and fostering an environment of open communication and mutual support.

Conclusion:

Embracing emotional intelligence involves understanding managing and leveraging emotions effectively in oneself and others.

By enhancing self-awareness and self-regulation individuals can navigate their emotions more effectively. Additionally building empathy and interpersonal skills enables individuals to establish stronger connections with others and build healthier relationships. With committed practice and continuous development individuals can embrace emotional intelligence leading to personal growth ilomproved well-being and success in various areas of life.

# 5

# Mastering Physical Abilities

"Mastering Physical Abilities" refers to the process of developing and honing physical skills, capabilities, and competencies to an advanced or expert level. This concept spans various domains, including sports, fitness, martial arts, dance, and other physical activities. Here's a detailed explanation:

1. Skill Development:

- Technique Refinement: Achieving mastery in physical abilities often involves refining and perfecting techniques. This includes improving form, coordination, balance, and precision in executing movements.

- Skill Acquisition: Learning and acquiring new skills are fundamental to mastery. It requires consistent practice, focused training, and the guidance of experienced coaches or mentors.

- Muscle Memory: Repetition is key to mastering physical skills. The more you practice a skill, the more ingrained it becomes in your muscle memory, allowing you to perform it effortlessly and with greater proficiency.

2. Physical Fitness:

- Strength: Building and mastering physical abilities often involves developing strength. This can be accomplished through weight training, bodyweight exercises, or resistance training.

- Endurance: Mastering physical abilities may require high levels of endurance, whether it's running a marathon, competing in an endurance sport, or excelling in physically demanding activities.

- Flexibility: Many physical activities necessitate flexibility, which can be improved through stretching and mobility exercises. Enhanced flexibility aids in preventing injuries and improving performance.

- Cardiovascular Fitness: A strong cardiovascular system is essential for sustaining physical abilities over time. It ensures efficient oxygen delivery to muscles and supports endurance.

3. Mental Toughness:

- Focus and Concentration: Mastery involves not only physical skills but also mental focus. Concentration and mindfulness during training and performance are crucial.

- Resilience: Developing resilience helps individuals overcome setbacks, injuries, or failures that may occur during the journey toward mastering physical abilities.

- Visualization: Mental imagery and visualization techniques can enhance performance by mentally rehearsing movements and scenarios, leading to improved execution.

4. Goal Setting and Monitoring:

- Setting Specific Goals: Clearly defined goals are essential for mastering physical abilities. These goals can be related to skill improvement, strength gains, or achieving specific milestones in a particular activity.

- Progress Tracking: Regularly monitoring your progress through metrics like performance records, fitness assessments, and skill evaluations is crucial for understanding where you stand and what areas need improvement.

5. Consistent Training:

- Dedication: Consistency in training is paramount. Mastery typically requires years of dedicated practice, often involving daily or regular training sessions.

- Periodization: Structured training plans, including periods of progressive overload, recovery, and skill refinement, can help individuals systematically work toward mastery.

6. Expert Guidance:

- Coaching and Mentorship: Working with experienced coaches or mentors can accelerate the path to mastery. They provide guidance, feedback, and personalized training plans.

- Peer Learning: Learning from peers who are also pursuing mastery can be motivating and provide opportunities for shared insights and improvement.

7. Patience and Perseverance:

- Long-Term Commitment: Achieving mastery in physical abilities is a long-term endeavor. It often involves overcoming plateaus, setbacks, and frustrations.

- Passion and Motivation: Maintaining a strong passion for the activity and staying motivated are essential for continued progress.

Part 1: Maintaining Physical Fitness

Maintaining physical fitness is crucial for leading a healthy and productive life. It involves engaging in regular physical activities and adopting a balanced and nutritious diet. Here we will delve deeper into the various components of physical fitness and how to optimize them.

1. Cardiovascular Endurance: Cardiovascular endurance refers to the ability of the heart blood vessels and lungs to supply oxygen to the working muscles over an extended period. Engaging in activities like running swimming cycling or brisk walking can help improve cardiovascular endurance. For example regular jogging or running for at least 30 minutes a day can strengthen the heart and improve lung capacity.

2. Muscular Strength: Muscular strength refers to the maximum force that a muscle or group of muscles can generate. Activities such as weightlifting resistance training or bodyweight exercises like push-ups squats and lunges can help increase muscular strength. For instance performing compound exercises like deadlifts and bench presses can target multiple muscle groups leading to significant strength gains.

3. Muscular Endurance: Muscular endurance is the ability of a muscle or group of muscles to perform repetitive contractions over an extended period without fatigue. Activities like high-repetition weightlifting circuit training or bodyweight exercises with minimal rests can improve muscular endurance. An example would be completing three sets of 15-20 repetitions of bicep curls with light weights.

4. Flexibility: Flexibility refers to the range of motion around a joint. Engaging in activities like stretching yoga or Pilates can enhance flexibility. For instance performing stretches that target major muscle groups such as hamstrings quadriceps and shoulders can improve overall flexibility.

5. Body Composition: Body composition refers to the ratio of fat mass to lean mass in the body. Maintaining a healthy body composition involves regular exercise and a balanced diet. For example incorporating resistance training and cardio exercises while consuming a diet consisting of lean proteins whole grains fruits and vegetables can help achieve a desirable body composition.

Part 2: Enhancing Coordination and Motor Skills

Coordination and motor skills are essential for performing any physical activity efficiently. They involve the synchronization of different body parts and the ability to execute movements with accuracy and precision. Let's explore some ways to enhance coordination and motor skills.

1. Balance: Maintaining good balance is crucial for overall coordination and stability. Activities like yoga tai chi or standing on one leg can improve balance. For example practicing balance poses like tree pose or warrior III in yoga can enhance balance and coordination.

2. Agility: Agility refers to the ability to change direction quickly and efficiently. Activities like ladder drills cone drills or plyometric exercises can enhance agility. For instance performing ladder drills involving quick footwork such as high knees lateral hops or fast feet can improve agility.

3. Hand-eye Coordination: Hand-eye coordination involves the ability to coordinate visual input with hand movements. Activities like catching and throwing a ball juggling or playing racket sports can improve hand-eye coordination. For example playing tennis or badminton requires precise timing and coordination between the eyes and hands.

4. Reaction Time: Reaction time refers to the speed at which an individual responds to a stimulus. Activities like reaction drills agility ladder drills or playing sports like table tennis or basketball can enhance reaction time. For instance engaging in reaction drills that involve reacting to visual or auditory cues can help improve reaction time.

## Part 3: Exploring Different Physical Activities

To master physical abilities it's essential to explore and engage in various physical activities. This helps in diversifying skills and developing a well-rounded fitness level. Here are some examples of different physical activities to consider:

1. Team Sports: Engaging in team sports like soccer basketball volleyball or rugby promotes teamwork coordination and cardiovascular fitness. Participating in team sports fosters communication enhances strategy development and boosts overall physical endurance.

2. Martial Arts: Practicing martial arts such as karate taekwondo or judo promotes self-discipline self-defense and physical fitness. Martial arts training improves coordination flexibility and self-confidence while teaching valuable skills for self-defense.

3. Dance: Dance forms like ballet hip-hop salsa or contemporary dance involve rhythmic movements coordination and flexibility. Dance enhances body control strength and artistic expression while providing an enjoyable way to stay fit.

4. Outdoor Activities: Outdoor activities like hiking rock climbing kayaking or cycling allow individuals to appreciate nature while improving cardiovascular fitness and strength. These activities provide opportunities for adventure exploration and a break from sedentary lifestyles.

5. Yoga and Pilates: Yoga and Pilates focus on strength flexibility

and mindfulness. These practices improve posture balance and core strength while reducing stress and promoting mental well-being.

6. Swimming: Swimming is a low-impact activity that exercises the entire body promotes cardiovascular fitness and improves muscle tone. It is a refreshing way to stay fit and it can be practiced both recreationally and competitively.

7. Outdoor Recreation: Engaging in activities like skateboarding surfing skiing or snowboarding not only provides a thrilling experience but also challenges coordination balance and muscular strength.

These are just a few examples and the list of physical activities available is extensive. It's crucial to choose activities that align with personal preferences and goals. Exploring different physical activities not only generates variety but also ensures the development of a diverse skill set.

In conclusion mastering physical abilities involves maintaining physical fitness enhancing coordination and motor skills and exploring various physical activities. By incorporating exercises that target cardiovascular endurance muscular strength muscular endurance flexibility and achieving a desirable body composition physical fitness can be maintained. Additionally by practicing balance agility hand-eye coordination and reaction time exercises coordination and motor skills can be improved. Finally exploring different physical activities such as team sports martial arts dance outdoor activities yoga and Pilates swimming and outdoor recreation can lead to a well-rounded fitness level and provide an enjoyable way to stay fit.

# 6

# Unleashing Creative Potential

Creativity is a vital skill that allows individuals to think outside the box explore new possibilities and develop innovative solutions. Unleashing creative potential involves tapping into one's imagination cultivating creative thinking skills and expressing oneself through various artistic mediums. In this Chapter we will explore each of these aspects in detail and provide examples to illustrate their significance in unleashing creative potential.

Tapping into Imagination and Innovation

Imagination plays a crucial role in creativity. It allows individuals to envision a world beyond the present imagine new ideas and explore diverse perspectives. By tapping into our imagination we can unlock our creative potential and push the boundaries of what is possible.

One way to tap into imagination is through brainstorming. Brainstorming involves generating a multitude of ideas without judgment or evaluation. For example let's imagine a group of designers tasked with creating a new product for a tech company. During a brainstorming session they might come up with various ideas such as a virtual reality headset that can transport users to different historical periods or a smartwatch that can analyze and improve sleep patterns.

Another way to tap into imagination is through visualization exercises. By actively visualizing a concept or scenario individuals can bring it to life in their minds. For instance a writer can close their eyes and imagine a character's appearance personality and backstory. This visualization process can spark creative ideas and bring depth to the character.

Cultivating Creative Thinking

Creative thinking involves the ability to generate unique ideas approach problems from different angles and make unexpected connections. It requires us to break away from conventional thinking patterns and embrace innovative solutions. Cultivating creative thinking skills is essential to unleashing our creative potential.

One effective technique for cultivating creative thinking is lateral thinking. Coined by Edward de Bono lateral thinking involves approaching problems from unconventional angles and thinking outside the box. For example let's say a marketing team is trying to promote a new soft drink. Instead of traditional advertisements they might employ guerrilla marketing tactics such as flash mobs or viral social media campaigns. This unconventional approach can capture people's attention and generate buzz around the product.

Another technique for cultivating creative thinking is mind mapping. Mind mapping involves visually organizing thoughts and ideas to establish connections and identify patterns. For instance an entrepreneur wanting to start a business can create a mind map that explores various potential industries market trends and personal interests. This visual representation can assist in identifying unique business opportunities and generating creative ideas for a successful venture.

By incorporating these techniques into our thinking processes we can stimulate our creative thinking skills and develop innovative solutions to various problems.

Expressing Yourself through Artistic Mediums

Artistic expression allows individuals to communicate their thoughts emotions and perspectives in a unique and personal way. By embracing artistic mediums such as painting writing music or dance individuals can unleash their creative potential and truly express themselves.

For example painting allows individuals to explore their emotions and experiences visually. An artist may use colors shapes and brushstrokes to convey their state of mind or communicate a particular message. Each stroke of the paintbrush carries personal meaning and enables the artist to express themselves in a way that words alone cannot.

Writing is another powerful medium for creative expression. Through storytelling individuals can create entire worlds develop complex characters and explore themes and ideas that resonate with them. Whether through fiction poetry or personal essays writing allows individuals to share their unique perspectives and experiences opening up possibilities for connection and understanding.

Music and dance provide avenues for emotional and physical expression. The rhythms melodies and movements in music and dance can convey a wide range of emotions and allow individuals to communicate without words. From classical compositions to contemporary choreography these artistic mediums provide limitless possibilities for creative expression.

By engaging with artistic mediums individuals can unleash their creative potential explore their identities and connect with others on a deep and emotional level.

Conclusion

Unleashing creative potential involves tapping into imagination and innovation cultivating creative thinking skills and expressing oneself through various artistic mediums. By harnessing the power of imagination individuals can envision new ideas and possibilities. The cultivation of creative thinking skills enables individuals to generate unique solutions and think outside the box. Through artistic expression individuals can communicate their thoughts emotions and perspectives in a way that connects with others on a profound level.

Whether through brainstorming visualization lateral thinking mind mapping painting writing music or dance there are numerous ways to unleash creative potential. The key is to embrace and nurture these skills in our lives. By doing so we can unlock our creativity tap into our unique perspectives and make a meaningful impact in various domains of life. Remember creativity knows no bounds and with practice and exploration anyone can unleash their creative potential.

# 7

# Building Effective Communication Skills

Communication is a vital aspect of human interaction and developing effective communication skills can significantly enhance our personal and professional lives. It involves conveying information ideas thoughts and feelings through various channels such as words gestures facial expressions and body language. In this Chapter we will explore the key components of effective communication including verbal and nonverbal communication active listening public speaking and overcoming communication barriers.

Verbal and Nonverbal Communication

Verbal communication refers to the use of spoken or written words to express thoughts or convey information. It includes the choice of words tone of voice volume and speed of delivery. The way we articulate our thoughts and feelings plays a crucial role in effective communication. For instance using clear and concise language avoiding jargon and adapting our vocabulary to the level of the audience can improve understanding and engagement.

Nonverbal communication on the other hand involves communicating without using words. It includes gestures facial expressions posture eye contact and body language. Nonverbal cues can convey emotions attitudes and intentions sometimes more effectively than words. For example a smile can indicate friendliness and openness while crossed arms may indicate defensiveness or resistance. Understanding and being mindful of nonverbal signals can enhance communication and promote trust between individuals.

Examples:

1. John is giving a presentation to his colleagues. He speaks clearly using appropriate language for the audience and maintains an engaging tone of voice throughout the presentation. He uses gestures and facial expressions to emphasize key points and maintain the audience's interest.

2. Sara is in a meeting with her team to discuss a challenging project. As she listens to her team members she maintains eye contact nods to show understanding and leans forward to indicate her interest. These nonverbal cues reassure her team members that she is actively engaged in the conversation and values their contributions.

Active Listening

Active listening is a fundamental aspect of effective communication. It involves fully focusing on the speaker comprehending the message and responding appropriately. Active listening requires concentration empathy and the ability to withhold judgment. By intentionally giving our full attention to the speaker we show respect and create an environment that encourages open and honest dialogue.

Examples:

1. During a conversation with his friend Mark actively listens by maintaining eye contact nodding to show understanding and asking thoughtful follow-up questions. He refrains from interrupting and provides supportive verbal and nonverbal cues to encourage his friend to express himself fully.

2. In a customer service role Emily practices active listening by giving her full attention to the customer even during difficult or challenging interactions. She paraphrases the customer's concerns to ensure she understands correctly and responds appropriately showing empathy and resolving issues effectively.

Public Speaking

Public speaking is the ability to deliver a compelling message to an audience in a clear confident and impactful manner. It is an essential skill in various professional settings such as presentations meetings or conferences. Effective public speaking involves proper preparation organizing ideas using visual aids if necessary and engaging the audience through effective delivery techniques.

Examples:

1. Alex is delivering a keynote speech at a conference. He begins by capturing the audience's attention with a strong opening statement and maintains their interest throughout by using storytelling techniques incorporating humor and varying

his speech pace and tone. He concludes with a powerful call to action that leaves a lasting impression on the audience.

2. Emma is leading a team meeting where she needs to present project updates. She prepares by creating a clear and concise presentation using visual aids such as slides and charts to enhance understanding. Emma engages her team by actively involving them in discussions encouraging their input and addressing any questions or concerns effectively.

Overcoming Communication Barriers

Communication barriers can hinder effective communication and lead to misunderstandings and conflicts. Recognizing and addressing these barriers is crucial for effective communication. Some common communication barriers include language barriers cultural differences distractions differences in perception and emotional barriers.

Examples:

1. Jenna is working on a project with a team member from a different country. They face language barriers which result in misinterpretations of instructions and expectations. To overcome this Jenna and her team member use visual aids such as diagrams or sketches to enhance understanding and clarify any confusion.

2. James and Sarah have differing perspectives on a particular issue. This difference in perception creates a communication barrier as both struggle to understand each other's points of view. To overcome this barrier they actively engage in open and honest dialogue using active listening skills empathy and

seeking common ground to bridge the gap.

In conclusion building effective communication skills is essential for both personal and professional success. Verbal and nonverbal communication active listening public speaking and overcoming communication barriers are key components of effective communication. By understanding and practicing these skills we can create meaningful connections foster productive relationships and ensure our messages are understood and appreciated. Developing strong communication skills takes time and effort but the benefits are invaluable.

# 8

# Harnessing Leadership Abilities

Leadership is a complex and multifaceted skill that plays a pivotal role in the success of individuals organizations and even societies. It involves guiding influencing and inspiring others towards a common goal all while demonstrating integrity empathy and strategic decision-making. Developing and harnessing these leadership abilities requires a deep understanding of the qualities of effective leaders the process of developing leadership skills and the art of leading and inspiring others. In this essay we will delve deeply into these aspects of leadership providing examples and insights along the way.

I. The Qualities of Effective Leaders:

Effective leaders possess a unique combination of qualities that enable them to lead with confidence clarity and authenticity. Here are some key qualities that define effective leaders:

1. Visionary: Effective leaders have a clear and compelling

vision of their desired future. They can articulate this vision to others inspiring and motivating them to work towards its realization. For example Steve Jobs the co-founder of Apple Inc had a visionary leadership style. He had a clear vision of creating user-friendly and innovative products that revolutionized the tech industry.

2. Integrity: Leaders who act with integrity gain the trust and respect of their followers. They uphold strong ethical principles remain true to their values and act transparently and honestly. An example of a leader who exemplified integrity is Nelson Mandela who stood up against apartheid in South Africa sacrificing his personal freedom for the greater good.

3. Emotional Intelligence: Effective leaders possess high emotional intelligence which allows them to understand and manage their own emotions while empathizing with others. They are adept at building strong relationships and are sensitive to the needs and concerns of their team members. Oprah Winfrey a renowned media personality is known for her emotional intelligence in connecting with her audience and understanding their emotions.

4. Resilience: Leaders face numerous challenges and setbacks along their journey. Effective leaders exhibit resilience by bouncing back from failures adapting to changes and leading by example. Elon Musk the CEO of Tesla and SpaceX has demonstrated resilience through difficult times in his businesses allowing him to lead his teams towards success.

5. Strategic Thinking: Effective leaders have a strategic mindset

enabling them to analyze complex situations anticipate future trends and make well-informed decisions. They consider both short-term and long-term implications ensuring the sustainability and growth of their organization. Indra Nooyi the former CEO of PepsiCo is recognized for her strategic thinking skills which helped transform the company's product portfolio and drive growth.

II. Developing Leadership Skills:

While certain leadership qualities may come naturally to some individuals most leadership skills can be developed and honed over time. Here are key steps to developing leadership skills:

1. Self-awareness: Developing self-awareness is a crucial first step in leadership development. Self-reflection seeking feedback from others and conducting assessments like personality tests can help individuals understand their strengths weaknesses and areas for improvement. By having a clear understanding of themselves individuals can leverage their strengths and address their development areas.

2. Continuous Learning: Effective leaders are lifelong learners constantly seeking new knowledge and skills to improve their leadership abilities. They read books attend seminars engage in online courses and seek mentorship to broaden their perspectives and stay abreast of industry trends. Bill Gates the co-founder of Microsoft is known for his dedication to continuous learning often reading more than 50 books in a year.

3. Experiential Learning: Leadership skills are best developed

through practical experience. Individuals can take on leadership roles within their organizations volunteer for leadership opportunities outside of work or participate in leadership development programs. These experiences allow leaders-in-training to apply theoretical knowledge to real-world situations and learn from both their successes and failures.

4. Relationship Building: Building strong relationships is a critical leadership skill. Leaders must develop effective communication skills actively listen provide feedback and cultivate relationships based on trust and mutual respect. By investing in relationships leaders can create a collaborative and supportive environment where individuals are motivated to perform their best. Jack Ma the co-founder of Alibaba Group is known for his exceptional relationship-building skills which have contributed to the success of his company.

5. Feedback and Reflection: Effective leaders actively seek feedback from colleagues mentors and team members. They use this feedback to identify areas for improvement and adjust their approach accordingly. Regular self-reflection and introspection also enable leaders to assess their actions and decisions fostering personal growth and development.

III. Leading and Inspiring Others:

Effective leaders not only cultivate their own leadership skills but also empower and inspire others to reach their full potential. Here are key practices for leading and inspiring others:

1. Setting Clear Expectations: Leaders must provide clear and

concise expectations to their team members. By setting goals defining roles and responsibilities and establishing performance criteria leaders create a sense of purpose and direction. Clear expectations help individuals stay focused aligned and motivated.

2. Communication and Transparency: Effective leaders communicate openly and transparently with their team members. They share relevant information provide regular updates and engage in active dialogue. Transparent communication builds trust and fosters a sense of belonging and involvement among team members.

3. Empowerment and Delegation: Leaders empower their team members by delegating tasks and responsibilities. By entrusting individuals with meaningful work and providing them with the necessary support and resources leaders foster autonomy accountability and personal growth. This approach encourages individuals to take ownership of their work and contribute their unique skills and perspectives.

4. Coaching and Mentoring: Leaders play a crucial role in developing the talents and potential of their team members. Through coaching and mentoring leaders provide guidance feedback and support to help individuals overcome challenges and enhance their performance. By investing in their team's development leaders create a pipeline of future leaders within their organization.

5. Recognizing and Celebrating Success: Effective leaders celebrate the achievements of their team members. They provide

recognition and rewards for exceptional performance fostering a positive and motivating work environment. By acknowledging and appreciating individual and team accomplishments leaders inspire their team members to strive for continued excellence.

Conclusion:

Harnessing leadership abilities requires a deep understanding of the qualities of effective leaders the process of developing leadership skills and the art of leading and inspiring others. Effective leaders possess qualities like vision integrity emotional intelligence resilience and strategic thinking. Developing leadership skills involve self-awareness continuous learning experiential learning relationship building and reflection. Leading and inspiring others necessitate setting clear expectations communication and transparency empowerment and delegation coaching and mentoring and recognizing and celebrating success.

By consciously cultivating these aspects of leadership individuals can harness their leadership abilities to make a positive impact in their personal and professional lives. Effective leaders have the potential to shape the future create positive change and inspire others to reach their full potential. As leadership is a journey of continuous growth and development individuals must commit to lifelong learning and improvement to become the best leaders they can be.

# 9

# Adapting to Change and Resilience

In a rapidly changing world the ability to adapt to change and display resilience is crucial for personal and professional success. Change is inherent in life; it can be gradual or sudden anticipated or unexpected. It can encompass various aspects such as transitions in work relationships health or even societal and global changes. Adapting to change requires flexibility resourcefulness and the ability to navigate through uncertainty. Resilience on the other hand is the capacity to bounce back from adversity maintain emotional stability and persevere through challenging situations. In this essay we will explore the concepts of adapting to change and resilience in depth examining their significance strategies for cultivation and providing examples to illustrate their practical application.

I. Embracing Change as an Opportunity:

Change is often perceived as disruptive unsettling or overwhelming. However it is essential to recognize that change also brings opportunities for growth personal development and the chance to explore new possibilities. Embracing change as an opportunity involves shifting our mindset and reframing our perspective. Here are some strategies to embrace change as an opportunity:

1. Maintaining a Growth Mindset: A growth mindset is the belief that one's abilities and intelligence can be developed through dedication and hard work. Individuals with a growth mindset perceive challenges as opportunities for learning and personal growth. They welcome change because it presents a chance to develop new skills acquire knowledge and expand their horizons.

2. Embracing the Unknown: Change often brings uncertainty and moves us outside our comfort zones. Embracing the unknown requires cultivating a sense of adventure and curiosity. By approaching change with a sense of openness we create the space for new experiences discoveries and personal transformation.

Example: Sarah a software developer was assigned to work on a new project using a programming language she was unfamiliar with. Initially she felt overwhelmed and doubted her abilities. However she embraced the change as an opportunity to learn and grow. Sarah took online courses sought guidance from colleagues and practiced programming tirelessly. Eventually she not only mastered the new language but her enhanced skill set opened up new career opportunities for her.

3. Developing Adaptability: Adaptability is the ability to adjust to new situations and challenges. Cultivating adaptability involves being flexible open-minded and willing to embrace change. It

requires being observant learning from our experiences and quickly adjusting our approach when necessary.

Example: Mark a sales manager had to adapt to a significant shift in the sales landscape due to the emergence of e-commerce. He recognized the need to move away from traditional sales techniques and embrace digital marketing strategies. Mark invested time in learning about social media marketing search engine optimization and online sales platforms. By adapting his sales approach to the digital era he was able to boost his team's performance and meet the evolving customer demands.

II. Building Mental and Emotional Resilience:

Resilience is the ability to overcome adversity bounce back from setbacks and maintain emotional well-being in the face of challenging situations. It is a skill that can be cultivated and strengthened through various strategies. Building mental and emotional resilience enables us to navigate through change with greater ease. Here are some strategies to build resilience:

1. Cultivating Self-Awareness: Self-awareness involves understanding our thoughts emotions and behavioral patterns. By becoming more aware of our strengths weaknesses and triggers we can develop healthier coping mechanisms and regulate our responses to adversity effectively.

Example: Maya a college student faced difficulties managing stress during exam periods which affected her performance. She started practicing mindfulness meditation to cultivate self-awareness. Through meditation she became more attuned to her thoughts and emotions allowing her to develop healthier coping mechanisms and manage exam-related stress more effectively.

2. Developing Problem-Solving Skills: Resilient individuals possess effective problem-solving skills allowing them to navigate difficulties with confidence. Developing problem-solving skills involves identifying the challenge breaking it down into manageable steps and finding creative solutions.

Example: Jake a small business owner faced a significant setback when his primary supplier abruptly discontinued a critical product. Instead of succumbing to the situation he focused on finding alternative suppliers negotiating new partnerships and even diversifying his product line. Through his problem-solving skills Jake was not only able to recover from the setback but also strengthen his business.

3. Building a Supportive Network: Having a reliable support system is vital for resilience. Surrounding ourselves with supportive friends family or mentors provides emotional encouragement practical advice and perspective during challenging times. Connecting with others who have experienced similar situations can also serve as a source of reassurance and inspiration.

Example: Rachel a divorcee with two young children faced emotional turmoil and financial instability following her divorce. She joined a support group for single parents where she found solidarity and received valuable guidance and emotional support. The support group's members shared their experiences offered practical advice and provided a safe space for Rachel to express her emotions. This support network helped Rachel navigate through the challenges she faced and build resilience.

III. Thriving in Challenging Situations:

Adapting to change and displaying resilience are not merely about surviving through difficulties; they also enable us to thrive in challenging situations. Thriving involves not only bouncing back but also leveraging adversity to grow stronger develop new skills and achieve personal fulfillment. Here are some strategies for thriving in challenging situations:

1. Cultivating a Positive Mindset: A positive mindset allows us to view challenges as opportunities for growth and maintain optimism during difficult times. Focusing on solutions practicing gratitude and reframing negative experiences can help foster a positive mindset.

Example: Emily an athlete suffered a career-ending injury. Although devastated she chose to view the setback as an opportunity to explore other passions. Emily pursued a degree in sports psychology allowing her to help other athletes overcome mental hurdles. By cultivating a positive mindset and seeing her injury as a catalyst for personal and professional growth Emily found fulfillment in a new career path.

2. Setting Realistic Goals: Setting realistic and attainable goals allows us to maintain motivation and a sense of purpose during challenging situations. By breaking larger goals into smaller manageable milestones we can maintain focus track progress and build momentum towards success.

Example: John an entrepreneur faced significant financial setbacks in his business due to market fluctuations. To remain motivated and inspired John set realistic goals for his business focusing on achievable milestones. By breaking down his long-term goals into smaller measurable targets John was able to build momentum and eventually turn his business around.

3. Practicing Self-Care: Self-care is essential for maintaining well-being replenishing energy and enhancing resilience. Engaging in activities that promote physical mental and emotional well-being allows us to manage stress effectively and thrive in challenging situations.

Example: Maria a busy professional faced burnout due to her demanding work schedule. She incorporated self-care practices into her daily routine making time for activities such as exercising practicing mindfulness and spending quality time with loved ones. By prioritizing self-care Maria experienced increased energy improved focus and a greater ability to navigate through challenging situations.

Conclusion:

Adapting to change and building resilience are essential skills in navigating the uncertainties of life. Embracing change as an opportunity allows us to grow explore new possibilities and expand our horizons. Building mental and emotional resilience strengthens our ability to bounce back from setbacks maintain emotional stability and thrive in challenging situations. By cultivating a growth mindset developing problem-solving skills building a support network and practicing self-care we gain the tools to adapt overcome adversity and thrive. Embracing change and building resilience are lifelong journeys but the effort we invest in cultivating these skills will undoubtedly lead to personal and professional fulfillment.

# 10

# Sustaining Motivation and Goal Setting

Sustaining motivation and goal setting are two crucial components of personal and professional development. They are interconnected and play a fundamental role in helping individuals achieve their desired outcomes. Let's delve deeper into each of these concepts:

1. Motivation:

Motivation refers to the internal or external factors that drive a person to take action, persist in their efforts, and achieve specific goals. It's the force that energizes, directs, and sustains behavior. Here are some key aspects of motivation:

- Intrinsic vs. Extrinsic Motivation: Intrinsic motivation comes from within and is driven by personal interests, enjoyment, or a sense of accomplishment. Extrinsic motivation, on the other hand, comes from external factors like rewards, recognition, or fear of punishment.

- Types of Motivation: Motivation can vary in intensity and

duration. Some people are highly motivated for short bursts of time (e.g., for a project deadline), while others are motivated over the long term (e.g., pursuing a career).

- Motivation Factors: Various factors influence motivation, including values, beliefs, needs, desires, and even societal or cultural influences. Understanding what motivates you personally is crucial for setting and achieving meaningful goals.

2. Goal Setting:

Goal setting is the process of identifying specific, measurable, achievable, relevant, and time-bound (SMART) objectives that you want to achieve. Effective goal setting provides direction, purpose, and a roadmap for your actions. Here's a more in-depth look at goal setting:

- Specific: Goals should be clear and well-defined. Vague objectives are challenging to pursue because they lack focus. Specific goals answer the questions of "what," "why," and "how."

- Measurable: You need to be able to track your progress and determine when you've achieved your goal. Measurable goals are quantifiable and allow you to assess your success.

- Achievable: Goals should be realistic and attainable. Setting unattainable goals can lead to frustration and demotivation. However, they should also stretch you beyond your comfort zone.

- Relevant: Goals should align with your values, long-term

objectives, and overall life plan. Relevance ensures that you stay committed and motivated to pursue them.

- Time-Bound: Set deadlines for your goals. This creates a sense of urgency and helps you allocate your time and resources effectively.

Connecting Sustaining Motivation and Goal Setting:

Sustaining motivation is critical for achieving long-term goals. While motivation can wane over time, effective goal setting can help maintain and even boost motivation. Here's how they are interconnected:

1. Motivation Drives Goal Setting: Your motivation provides the initial impetus for setting goals. When you're motivated, you're more likely to identify what you want to achieve and why it's essential.

2. Goals Provide Motivation: Goals create a clear vision of your desired outcome, making it easier to stay motivated. Progress toward achieving your goals can be a powerful source of motivation.

3. Regular Goal Review: Revisiting your goals periodically helps sustain motivation. You can assess your progress, adjust your approach, and remind yourself why you set those goals in the first place.

4. Adaptability: Sustaining motivation often requires adjusting your goals as circumstances change. Being flexible and adapt-

able while maintaining your motivation can lead to continued success.

5. Celebrate Achievements: Recognize and celebrate your achievements along the way. This boosts motivation by providing a sense of accomplishment and reminding you of your progress.

**Understanding Motivation and its Importance:**

Motivation is the driving force that pushes us to take action, persevere through challenges, and achieve our goals. It's the spark that ignites our enthusiasm and determination. Motivation can be internal, stemming from personal values, passions, and a sense of purpose, or external, influenced by rewards, recognition, or pressure.

Importance of Motivation:

- Goal Initiation: Motivation prompts us to set goals and start working towards them. Without motivation, we might lack the energy and desire to begin.

- Goal Persistence: Challenges and setbacks are inevitable, but motivation helps us persevere. It keeps us focused on the long-term rewards rather than giving up due to short-term difficulties.

- Effort and Performance: Motivated individuals tend to invest more effort into their tasks, leading to improved performance and better results.

- Adaptability: Motivated people are more open to learning and adapting. They embrace change and see it as an opportunity for growth.

- Personal Satisfaction: Achieving goals driven by motivation brings a sense of accomplishment and personal satisfaction, boosting overall well-being.

**Setting SMART Goals for Success:**

SMART is an acronym that stands for Specific, Measurable, Achievable, Relevant, and Time-bound. Applying these criteria to goal setting enhances the chances of success.

SMART Goals Explained:

- Specific: Define your goal clearly and concisely. Avoid vague statements and focus on the precise outcome you want to achieve.

- Measurable: Set criteria to measure your progress and determine when the goal is achieved. Quantify your goal whenever possible.

- Achievable: Ensure that your goal is realistic and attainable given your resources, skills, and circumstances. A challenging goal is good, but an impossible one can lead to frustration.

- Relevant: Your goal should align with your values, aspirations, and broader objectives. It should contribute to your overall growth and well-being.

- Time-bound: Set a deadline for your goal. Having a time frame creates a sense of urgency and helps you manage your time effectively.

Strategies for Maintaining Motivation:

Maintaining motivation over the long term can be challenging, but certain strategies can help you stay inspired and committed.

**Motivation Maintenance Strategies:**

- Break Down Goals: Divide larger goals into smaller, manageable tasks. Achieving these milestones provides a continuous sense of accomplishment.

- Visualize Success: Imagine the satisfaction and benefits of achieving your goal. Visualization reinforces your motivation and helps you stay focused.

- Positive Self-Talk: Replace self-doubt with positive affirmations. Encourage yourself with constructive thoughts and beliefs.

- Reward Yourself: Celebrate your achievements, even the small ones. Rewards provide a sense of recognition and serve as positive reinforcement.

- Seek Support: Share your goals with friends, family, or mentors who can provide encouragement, accountability, and guidance.

- Stay Flexible: Adapt your goals as needed. Life is dynamic, and being flexible prevents demotivation due to unexpected changes.

- Stay Inspired: Read books, watch videos, or interact with people who inspire you. Surround yourself with positivity and motivational content.

In conclusion, understanding motivation, setting SMART goals, and employing strategies to maintain motivation are integral to achieving success and personal growth. A strong foundation of motivation, combined with well-defined goals and effective strategies, can propel you toward realizing your aspirations and becoming the best version of yourself.

# II

# Part Two

# 11

# Time Management and Productivity

In today's fast-paced world, time management and productivity have become critical skills for personal and professional success. Effective time management allows individuals to make the most of their available time, accomplishing tasks efficiently and reducing stress. In this comprehensive exploration, we will delve into various techniques, strategies, and real-world examples to understand and master time management and productivity.

Section 1: Techniques for Effective Time Management

Time management is not about squeezing as many tasks as possible into your day; it's about making conscious choices about how to spend your time to achieve your goals. Let's explore some techniques:

1.1. Setting Priorities:

- Time management begins with identifying your most important tasks. The Eisenhower Matrix, for example, categorizes tasks into four quadrants: urgent and important, important but not urgent, urgent but not important, and neither urgent nor important. By focusing on what's important, you allocate your time wisely.

- Example: Imagine a project manager who uses this matrix to decide between addressing a critical client issue (urgent and important) and attending a routine team meeting (important but not urgent).

1.2. Time Blocking:

- Time blocking involves scheduling specific blocks of time for particular tasks. This method helps reduce multitasking and ensures you allocate dedicated time for focused work.
- Example: A writer may block out the morning hours for writing Chapters, the afternoon for research, and the evening for editing.

1.3. Pomodoro Technique:

- This technique breaks work into intervals, typically 25 minutes of focused work followed by a 5-minute break. After completing four cycles, you take a more extended break. It enhances productivity and maintains concentration.
- Example: A student uses the Pomodoro Technique to study for exams, finding that short, focused bursts help retain information.

1.4. Time Tracking:

- Keeping a time log to record how you spend your day can provide valuable insights into where your time goes. You can identify time-wasting activities and make informed adjustments.

- Example: An office worker uses time tracking to discover they spend an excessive amount of time checking emails, leading them to set specific email-checking intervals.

1.5. Avoiding Multitasking:

- Contrary to popular belief, multitasking often decreases productivity. Focusing on one task at a time allows for better concentration and quality of work.
- Example: A manager realizes that they make fewer errors and complete tasks faster when they give their full attention to each task separately.

Section 2: Strategies for Prioritizing Tasks and Avoiding Procrastination

Prioritizing tasks and avoiding procrastination are integral to effective time management. Let's examine strategies to make these practices a habit:

2.1. Eisenhower's Urgent-Important Matrix:

- We revisit this matrix as a tool for systematically categorizing tasks. The key is to address urgent and important tasks first, followed by the others.
- Example: A business owner uses this matrix to decide whether to address a sudden equipment breakdown (urgent and important) or schedule regular employee training (important but not urgent).

2.2. The 2-Minute Rule:

- If a task can be completed in two minutes or less, do it immediately. This rule helps clear small tasks that can otherwise accumulate.

- Example: An executive responds to short emails and approves minor requests immediately, reducing email clutter and fostering quicker decision-making.

2.3. Eat the Frog:

- Coined by Brian Tracy, this concept suggests tackling your most challenging or unpleasant task first thing in the morning. Completing the 'frog' gives you a sense of accomplishment.
- Example: A student starts their day with the most challenging subject to ensure they devote their freshest hours to it.

2.4. The Zeigarnik Effect:

- This psychological principle states that people tend to remember and worry about uncompleted or interrupted tasks. To avoid this, aim to finish what you start.
- Example: A writer avoids starting multiple Chapters simultaneously and ensures they complete one before moving on to the next.

2.5. Overcoming Procrastination:

- Procrastination often stems from fear, perfectionism, or lack of motivation. Identifying the root cause is crucial in overcoming it. Techniques like setting specific deadlines, breaking tasks into smaller steps, and finding accountability partners can help.
- Example: A graphic designer addresses procrastination by breaking complex design projects into smaller, manageable tasks with set deadlines.

Section 3: Balancing Work, Personal Life, and Self-Improvement

Achieving a harmonious balance between work, personal life, and self-improvement is essential for long-term well-being. Let's explore strategies for maintaining this balance:

3.1. Time Audit:

- Conduct a comprehensive analysis of how you spend your time. Identify areas where you can reallocate time for self-improvement and personal life.
- Example: A manager realizes they're spending excessive time at work and decides to delegate more tasks to create time for family and hobbies.

3.2. The 80/20 Principle (Pareto Principle):

- This principle suggests that 80% of results come from 20% of efforts. Identify your most productive hours and allocate them to high-impact tasks, leaving more time for personal life.
- Example: A salesperson focuses their peak energy hours on the most critical sales calls, freeing up time to spend with family.

3.3. Effective Delegation:

- Learning to delegate tasks and responsibilities at work can free up time for self-improvement and personal life. It also empowers team members.
- Example: A business owner delegates administrative tasks to an assistant, allowing them to focus on strategic planning and spend more time with their children.

3.4. Boundaries and Time Management:

- Setting clear boundaries between work and personal life is vital. Establish specific working hours and stick to them. Avoid work-related activities during personal time.

- Example: A freelancer ensures they stop working at 6 PM every day to spend quality time with family, setting a firm boundary between work and personal life.

3.5. Self-Care and Self-Improvement Routine:

- Prioritize self-care activities like exercise, meditation, reading, or learning new skills. Allocate time for self-improvement to grow personally and professionally.
- Example: A professional dedicates an hour each morning to personal development, reading books, and acquiring new skills before starting work.

Real-World Examples of Effective Time Management and Productivity:

- Elon Musk: The CEO of Tesla and SpaceX is known for his rigorous time management. He breaks his day into five-minute slots, which allows him to allocate time efficiently across multiple companies and projects.

- Marie Kondo: The organization guru and author of "The Life-Changing Magic of Tidying Up" emphasizes the importance of decluttering and organizing as a way to free up mental and physical space, ultimately improving productivity and well-being.

- Warren Buffett: The billionaire investor follows the principle of "less is more." He's famous for his 5/25 rule, where he lists his top 25 goals and then focuses on the top five, avoiding the rest until the first five are achieved.

- Bill Gates: The co-founder of Microsoft is known for his love of reading. He dedicates a significant portion of his time to reading books, which he considers crucial for gaining knowledge and insights.

- Tim Ferriss: The author of "The 4-Hour Workweek" advocates for maximizing efficiency and outsourcing tasks. His approach emphasizes focusing on what truly matters while delegating or eliminating the rest.

In conclusion, mastering time management and productivity involves a combination of techniques, strategies, and self-awareness. By setting priorities, avoiding procrastination, and striking a balance between work, personal life, and self-improvement, individuals can achieve their goals and lead more fulfilling lives. The real-world examples of successful individuals serve as inspiration and practical guidance for implementing these principles effectively.

# 12

# Financial Literacy and Wealth Building

Financial literacy plays a critical role in individual and societal well-being. It encompasses the knowledge skills and tools necessary to make informed decisions about personal finance including budgeting saving investing and understanding the complexities of the financial system. In this Chapter we will delve deeply into the importance of financial education explore various budgeting and saving strategies and discuss investment and wealth-building principles.

Section 1: The Importance of Financial Education

1.1 Empowerment and Independence:

Financial education empowers individuals to take control of their financial lives. It equips them with the knowledge and skills needed to make sound financial decisions thereby promoting personal independence and financial well-being.

1.2 Mitigating Risks:

Financial literacy provides individuals with the ability to identify and mitigate financial risks. It helps them navigate potential pitfalls such as falling prey to scams accumulating excessive debt or making hasty investment decisions without proper evaluation.

1.3 Confidence in Financial Decision-making:

Without a solid foundation in financial literacy individuals may feel overwhelmed when faced with life-changing financial decisions. Sound financial education instills confidence in decision-making allowing individuals to assess options effectively and choose those that align with their long-term goals.

1.4 Promoting Economic Stability:

Improved financial literacy at the societal level contributes to overall economic stability. When individuals understand concepts such as inflation interest rates and the impact of market forces on their finances they make informed choices that stabilize their personal economies and collectively the economy as a whole.

Section 2: Budgeting and Saving Strategies

2.1 Building a Budget:

Budgeting is the cornerstone of financial stability. It involves allocating income to various expenses savings and investing. By creating a budget individuals can effectively manage their money track spending patterns and identify areas for improvement.

Example: John wants to create a budget. He starts by listing his monthly income from his job rental property and other sources. Then he tracks all his essential expenses such as rent utilities and groceries. Finally he allocates a portion of his income toward savings and investments ensuring that he is setting aside funds for future goals.

2.2 Tracking Expenses:

Monitoring and categorizing expenses is crucial for financial success. It helps identify unnecessary expenditures and encourages individuals to prioritize their spending habits.

Example: Sarah keeps a record of all her expenses on a smartphone app. At the end of each month she reviews her spending patterns and realizes she is spending more on dining out than she anticipated. She decides to reduce her restaurant expenses and reallocate those funds towards her savings goals.

2.3 Emergency Funds:

Creating an emergency fund is an essential aspect of financial planning. It provides a safety net during unforeseen circumstances such as a medical emergency or job loss.

Example: Mark decides to save six months' worth of living expenses in an emergency fund. By setting aside a portion of his income each month Mark gradually builds a financial cushion that protects him during unexpected events.

2.4 Automating Savings:

Automating savings is an effective strategy to ensure consistent savings habits. By setting up automatic transfers from their checking to their savings account individuals remove the temptation to spend money that should be saved.

Example: Lisa sets up an automatic transfer of $100 from her checking account to her savings account every payday. This way she ensures that she consistently saves a portion of her income without having to remember to do so manually.

Section 3: Investment and Wealth Building Principles

3.1 Diversification:

Diversification is a critical investment principle that involves spreading investments across different asset classes sectors and geographical regions. It helps mitigate risks and increase the potential for returns.

Example: Andrew diversifies his investment portfolio by allocating a portion to stocks bonds real estate and mutual funds. By doing so he reduces the impact of a single investment's performance on his overall portfolio.

3.2 Compound Interest:

Compound interest is an essential concept in wealth building. It allows individuals to earn interest on both the initial investment and the accumulated interest over time leading to exponential growth.

Example: Rachel invests $5000 in a compound interest account with an annual interest rate of 5%. After 10 years her investment would have grown to approximately $8235 without any additional contributions.

3.3 Risk Tolerance:

Understanding risk tolerance is fundamental when making investment decisions. It involves assessing an individual's willingness and ability to endure market volatility and potential losses.

Example: David carefully assesses his risk tolerance by considering his financial goals investment timeframe and emotional tolerance for market fluctuations. Based on this assessment he chooses investment vehicles that align with his risk tolerance.

3.4 Long-Term Investing:

A long-term investment approach is essential for wealth building. It allows individuals to harness the power of compounding and ride out short-term market fluctuations.

Example: Emma adopts a long-term investment strategy by investing in a diversified portfolio of low-cost index funds. Rather than reactively buying and selling investments based on short-term market trends she focuses on her long-term financial goals.

Conclusion:

Financial literacy is crucial for individuals to take control of their financial futures. Understanding personal finance concepts budgeting strategies and investment principles empowers individuals to make informed decisions that contribute to their economic stability and long-term wealth building. By promoting financial education and implementing sound financial habits individuals can embark on a path toward financial success and achieve their life goals.

# 13

# Health and Well-being

In a fast-paced and often demanding world, maintaining one's health and well-being is essential for a fulfilling life. This comprehensive exploration delves deeply into strategies for achieving and sustaining physical and mental well-being. We'll cover various aspects, including maintaining physical health through diet and exercise, managing mental health and stress, and the significance of self-care and work-life balance.

Section 1: Strategies for Maintaining Physical Health Through Diet and Exercise

Physical health is the cornerstone of overall well-being. A balanced diet and regular exercise play pivotal roles in ensuring good health. Let's explore effective strategies:

1.1. Balanced Diet:

- A balanced diet consists of a variety of nutrients, including carbohydrates, proteins, fats, vitamins, and minerals. It's essential for energy, growth, and overall health.

- Explanation: Your body needs carbohydrates for energy, proteins for muscle and tissue repair, fats for cell function, and various vitamins and minerals for numerous bodily functions.

1.2. Portion Control:

- Controlling portion sizes helps prevent overeating and maintain a healthy weight. Understanding appropriate portion sizes is key to a balanced diet.
- Explanation: Smaller portions prevent excess calorie intake, which can lead to weight gain and various health issues like obesity and diabetes.

1.3. Hydration:

- Staying adequately hydrated is vital for bodily functions. Water helps transport nutrients, regulate body temperature, and remove waste.
- Explanation: Dehydration can lead to fatigue, headaches, and impaired cognitive function. Drinking enough water supports physical health.

1.4. Nutrient-Rich Foods:

- Focus on consuming nutrient-dense foods like fruits, vegetables, lean proteins, and whole grains. These foods provide essential vitamins and minerals.
- Explanation: Nutrient-rich foods supply vital nutrients with fewer calories, promoting overall health and preventing nutrient deficiencies.

1.5. Regular Exercise:

- Regular physical activity is crucial for maintaining physical health. It strengthens muscles, improves cardiovascular health, and enhances flexibility.

- Explanation: Exercise increases blood flow, which supports heart health, and stimulates the release of endorphins, promoting mental well-being.

1.6. Creating a Fitness Routine:

- Establishing a consistent exercise routine helps maintain physical health. Incorporate aerobic, strength, and flexibility exercises into your plan.
- Explanation: A well-rounded fitness routine improves overall health, reduces the risk of chronic diseases, and enhances physical performance.

1.7. Sleep and Recovery:

- Adequate sleep is essential for physical health. It allows the body to rest, repair tissues, and recharge for the day ahead.
- Explanation: Poor sleep can lead to physical and mental health issues, including fatigue, weakened immunity, and increased stress.

1.8. Preventive Health Measures:

- Regular health check-ups and screenings are essential for early detection of health issues. Vaccinations and health monitoring can prevent diseases.
- Explanation: Preventive measures can identify and address health concerns before they become severe, ensuring better overall health.

## Section 2: Mental Health and Stress Management Techniques

Mental health is as crucial as physical health, and managing stress is paramount. Here are strategies to support mental well-being:

2.1. Recognizing Mental Health:

- Acknowledging the importance of mental health is the first step. Mental health includes emotional, psychological, and social well-being.
- Explanation: Mental health affects thoughts, feelings, and behavior, influencing how individuals handle stress, relate to others, and make choices.

2.2. Stress Awareness:

- Identifying stressors and their impact on mental health is crucial. Stress can manifest physically and emotionally.
- Explanation: Chronic stress can lead to anxiety, depression, and physical health problems, emphasizing the need for stress management.

2.3. Stress Management Techniques:

- Various techniques can help manage stress, including mindfulness, meditation, deep breathing exercises, and progressive muscle relaxation.
- Explanation: These techniques calm the mind, reduce stress hormones, and promote relaxation and mental clarity.

2.4. Seeking Support:

- Sharing concerns with trusted friends, family, or mental health professionals can provide valuable support. Seeking help is a sign of strength.
- Explanation: Talking to someone can offer perspective, guidance, and emotional support during challenging times.

2.5. Practicing Mindfulness:

- Mindfulness involves staying present in the moment without judgment. It reduces stress and enhances well-being.
- Explanation: Mindfulness practices, like meditation, improve focus, reduce anxiety, and promote mental resilience.

2.6. Self-compassion:

- Being kind to oneself, especially in difficult situations, is crucial for mental health. Self-compassion fosters self-acceptance and resilience.
- Explanation: Self-criticism can exacerbate mental health issues, while self-compassion promotes emotional well-being.

2.7. Healthy Relationships:

- Nurturing positive relationships with friends and family can enhance mental health. Social connections provide emotional support.
- Explanation: Isolation and loneliness can contribute to mental health problems, while strong relationships offer a sense of belonging and well-being.

2.8. Professional Help:

- When mental health issues persist or worsen, seeking professional help, such as therapy or counseling, is essential.
- Explanation: Mental health professionals can provide guidance, coping strategies, and treatment for various mental health conditions.

Section 3: The Importance of Self-Care and Work-Life Balance

Self-care and work-life balance are critical components of

overall well-being. They ensure that individuals prioritize their physical and mental health:

3.1. Self-Care Practices:

- Self-care involves intentional actions to care for one's physical, mental, and emotional well-being. It includes activities like exercise, relaxation, and hobbies.
- Explanation: Self-care prevents burnout, reduces stress, and promotes a sense of fulfillment and happiness.

3.2. Setting Boundaries:

- Establishing clear boundaries between work and personal life is essential. Overworking can lead to burnout and negatively impact mental health.
- Explanation: Boundaries protect personal time, allowing individuals to relax, recharge, and spend time with loved ones.

3.3. Time Management:

- Effective time management ensures that individuals allocate time for work, self-care, and personal life. It reduces stress and enhances balance.
- Explanation: Proper time management prevents work from encroaching on personal time, fostering a healthier work-life balance.

3.4. Prioritizing Personal Life:

- Prioritizing personal life over work is crucial for well-being. Personal time allows for relaxation, hobbies, and spending time with loved ones.
- Explanation: Neglecting personal life can lead to increased stress, strained relationships, and a diminished sense of fulfill-

ment.

3.5. Work-Life Balance Strategies:

- Strategies like setting work hours, taking regular breaks, and unplugging from work-related technology can improve work-life balance.
- Explanation: A balanced work-life ratio leads to increased job satisfaction, reduced stress, and better overall well-being.

3.6. Mindful Technology Use:

- Mindful use of technology involves limiting screen time and being conscious of the impact of digital devices on well-being.
- Explanation: Excessive technology use can contribute to stress, sleep disturbances, and decreased personal time. Mindful use promotes balance.

Real-World Examples of Health and Well-being:

1. Michelle Obama's "Let's Move!" Campaign: As First Lady, Michelle Obama launched the "Let's Move!" campaign, which aimed to combat childhood obesity by promoting physical activity and healthy eating. This initiative highlighted the importance of diet and exercise in maintaining physical health.

2. Meditation and Mindfulness Apps: Apps like Headspace and Calm have gained popularity for their role in promoting mental well-being through guided meditation and mindfulness practices.

3. Arianna Huffington's Thrive Global: The founder of The Huffington Post launched Thrive Global, a platform dedicated

to well-being and productivity. This platform emphasizes the importance of work-life balance, sleep, and mental health in achieving success and happiness.

4. Employee Wellness Programs: Many companies now offer employee wellness programs that include fitness facilities, mental health resources, and stress management tools to promote the well-being of their employees.

In conclusion, maintaining health and well-being is a multifaceted endeavor that encompasses physical health through diet and exercise, mental health through stress management, and self-care practices. Prioritizing self-care and achieving a work-life balance are equally important for overall well-being. Real-world examples demonstrate how individuals and organizations are prioritizing health and well-being, and these strategies can serve as a foundation for readers seeking to enhance their own well-being.

# 14

# Networking and Relationship Building

Building and nurturing professional and personal relationships are essential skills in today's interconnected world. Whether it is in our careers or personal lives the ability to connect with others build trust and maintain strong relationships can open up countless opportunities. In this chapter we will explore effective networking techniques as well as conflict resolution and communication strategies in relationships.

Effective Networking Techniques:

Networking is a powerful tool that can help us expand our professional circles gain new business opportunities and enhance our careers. Here are some effective techniques for networking:

1. Identify Your Goals: Before attending a networking event or connecting with someone it is important to identify your goals. Are you looking for new job opportunities seeking potential clients or aiming to connect with industry experts? Having a clear understanding of what you want to achieve will help you

focus your efforts and make meaningful connections.

2. Attend Events and Join Communities: Attend conferences seminars and social gatherings related to your field. These events provide an excellent opportunity to meet new people who share your interests. Additionally joining professional associations or online communities can connect you with like-minded individuals and expand your network.

3. Be Authentic and Genuine: Effective networking is not about collecting as many business cards as possible; it's about building genuine connections. Be authentic approachable and interested in others. Ask open-ended questions and actively listen to what people have to say. Showing genuine interest in others allows for deeper connections and fosters trust.

4. Follow Up and Stay Connected: After networking events it is essential to follow up with the people you have met. Send personalized emails or LinkedIn messages and express your gratitude for the conversation. Additionally stay connected by sharing valuable resources or attending industry events together. Regular interaction helps nurture relationships and keeps you on their radar.

Conflict Resolution and Communication in Relationships:

Building relationships is not just about creating connections; it also involves sustaining healthy communication and effectively resolving conflicts. Here are some strategies to handle conflicts and enhance communication in relationships:

1. Active Listening: Effective communication begins with

active listening. When someone is expressing their thoughts or concerns give them your full attention and maintain eye contact. Paraphrase their statements to ensure understanding and avoid interrupting. Active listening demonstrates respect and encourages open dialogue.

2. Open and Honest Communication: Healthy relationships are built on trust and openness. It is important to communicate openly and honestly. Express your thoughts and feelings clearly using "I" statements rather than blaming or criticizing the other person. This way you create a safe space for open conversation without becoming defensive.

For example instead of saying "You never listen to me say "I feel unheard when I don't see active engagement during our conversations."

3. Managing Conflict: Conflicts are bound to arise in any relationship but it is how we manage them that determines the strength and growth of the relationship. When conflicts occur take a calm and assertive approach. Find a suitable time and place to discuss the issue and ensure that both parties have an opportunity to share their perspective. Use active listening skills to understand each other's point of view and work towards finding mutually acceptable solutions.

4. Empathy and Understanding: To effectively resolve conflicts it is crucial to practice empathy and understanding. Put yourself in the other person's shoes and try to understand their feelings and concerns. This helps create a supportive environment where both parties feel heard and validated.

5. Seeking Mediation: In some situations conflicts may become difficult to resolve independently. In such cases it can be beneficial to seek mediation from a neutral third party such as a counselor or mediator. Mediators can facilitate the conversation help both parties feel heard and guide them towards finding a resolution.

In conclusion networking and relationship building are invaluable skills that can enhance both our personal and professional lives. Effective networking techniques enable us to expand our connections while conflict resolution and communication strategies foster healthy and meaningful relationships. By being authentic actively listening and practicing open and honest communication we can build and nurture relationships that support our personal growth and success.

# 15

# Mindfulness and Meditation

In today's fast-paced and demanding world many individuals find themselves overwhelmed and struggling to maintain a sense of balance and mental well-being. Mindfulness and meditation offer powerful tools and practices that can help alleviate stress enhance mental clarity and promote overall well-being. In this Chapter we will explore the benefits of mindfulness and meditation and provide practical guidance for incorporating these practices into your daily life.

Benefits of Mindfulness and Meditation:

1. Stress Reduction: One of the primary benefits of mindfulness and meditation is their ability to reduce stress. By focusing your attention on the present moment and letting go of worries or anxieties about the future or past mindfulness helps break the cycle of stress and promotes a sense of calm.

2. Improved Mental Clarity and Focus: Regular practice of mindfulness and meditation enhances mental clarity concentration

and focus. By training the mind to be present and aware you develop the ability to focus on tasks at hand and maintain better cognitive performance.

3. Emotional Well-being: Mindfulness and meditation can have a positive impact on emotional well-being by increasing self-awareness and promoting emotional regulation. These practices cultivate a sense of equanimity and help individuals develop a greater understanding and acceptance of their emotions.

4. Better Sleep: Mindfulness and meditation are powerful tools for promoting relaxation and improving sleep quality. By calming the mind and reducing anxiety these practices help individuals experience deeper and more restful sleep resulting in increased energy levels and improved overall health.

Practical Guidance for Incorporating Mindfulness into Daily Life:

1. Start with Short Sessions: Begin by dedicating a few minutes each day to mindfulness practice. Sit comfortably in a quiet space close your eyes and focus on your breath. Observe the sensations of your breath as it enters and leaves your body allowing your mind to settle into a present-moment awareness.

2. Engage in Mindful Eating: Use mealtimes as an opportunity to practice mindfulness. Slow down and pay attention to the flavors textures and sensations of each bite. Be fully present and savor the experience. This practice can help cultivate a healthier relationship with food and prevent overeating.

3. Take Mindful Breaks: Incorporate short mindfulness breaks

throughout your day. Pause for a few minutes to focus on your breath or simply observe the sights sounds and sensations around you. These breaks can help you become more grounded and present amidst the busyness of life.

4. Mindful Walking: Transform your daily walks into a mindful practice. Pay attention to the sensation of each step the feeling of the ground beneath your feet and the movement of your body. Engaging in mindful walking can help you connect with nature reduce stress and improve overall well-being.

5. Use Mindfulness Apps: Several apps offer guided mindfulness meditations and practices. These apps can be a helpful tool for beginners or those seeking guidance. Popular options include Headspace Calm and Insight Timer. Experiment with different apps to find one that resonates with you.

Stress Reduction and Mental Clarity through Meditation:

1. Set Aside Time for Practice: Dedicate a specific time each day for meditation. Choose a quiet space where you won't be disturbed. Start with 5-10 minutes and gradually increase the duration as you become more comfortable.

2. Choose a Technique: There are various meditation techniques including focused attention loving-kindness and body scan meditation. Experiment with different techniques to find one that suits you best. Focused attention meditation involves focusing your attention on a single point such as your breath a mantra or a candle flame. Loving-kindness meditation involves cultivating feelings of compassion and love towards yourself and others. Body scan meditation involves systematically paying

attention to each part of your body.

3. Cultivate Non-Judgmental Awareness: During meditation it's common for the mind to wander. When this happens gently bring your attention back to the present moment without judgment or self-criticism. Recognize that wandering thoughts are natural and part of the process.

4. Create a Sacred Space: Designate a specific area in your home as a meditation space. Decorate it with objects that inspire calmness and tranquility such as candles plants or meaningful artwork. Having a dedicated space can enhance your meditation experience and serve as a reminder of the importance of self-care.

Conclusion:

Mindfulness and meditation offer numerous benefits for stress reduction enhanced mental clarity and overall well-being. By incorporating mindfulness into daily life and dedicating time for regular meditation practice individuals can experience significant improvements in their mental emotional and physical health. Remember the journey of mindfulness and meditation is a personal one and finding what works best for you may involve some experimentation and exploration. Embrace the practice with an open mind and enjoy the transformative effects it can have on your life.

# 16

# Innovation and Problem Solving

Innovation and problem-solving are critical drivers of progress and success in today's dynamic world. This comprehensive exploration delves deeply into the art of encouraging creative problem-solving, equipping individuals with tools and methods for fostering innovation, and drawing inspiration from real-world examples of innovative thinkers.

Section 1: Encouraging Creative Problem-Solving

Creative problem-solving is an invaluable skill that enables individuals to tackle complex challenges with imaginative and innovative solutions. Here are strategies to encourage and enhance this skill:

1.1. Embracing a Growth Mindset:
 - Cultivating a growth mindset fosters the belief that abilities and intelligence can be developed through effort and learning. This mindset encourages individuals to approach problems with enthusiasm and resilience.

- Explanation: A growth mindset encourages individuals to embrace challenges and view failures as opportunities for learning and growth.

1.2. Divergent Thinking:

- Divergent thinking involves generating a multitude of ideas and solutions. Techniques like brainstorming and mind mapping are effective for divergent thinking.
- Explanation: Divergent thinking helps individuals explore various angles and possibilities when addressing a problem.

1.3. Interdisciplinary Collaboration:

- Collaboration among individuals with diverse backgrounds and expertise often leads to creative solutions. Bringing together different perspectives sparks innovation.
- Explanation: Collaborative problem-solving draws from a variety of knowledge areas and fosters unique insights and approaches.

1.4. Design Thinking:

- Design thinking is a problem-solving approach that prioritizes empathy, ideation, and prototyping. It encourages a human-centered perspective to tackle complex issues.
- Explanation: Design thinking involves understanding the needs and experiences of users, brainstorming solutions, and rapidly prototyping and testing ideas.

1.5. Failure as a Stepping Stone:

- Embracing failure as part of the problem-solving process is essential. Each failure provides valuable lessons and brings you closer to innovative solutions.

- Explanation: Many groundbreaking innovations have arisen from multiple failures and iterations.

Section 2: Tools and Methods for Fostering Innovation

Innovation is not a spontaneous act but a systematic process. Utilizing tools and methods can enhance the innovation journey:

2.1. SWOT Analysis:
- SWOT (Strengths, Weaknesses, Opportunities, Threats) analysis helps individuals and organizations identify their internal strengths and weaknesses, as well as external opportunities and threats. This analysis informs strategic decision-making.
- Explanation: A SWOT analysis provides a structured approach to understanding the current state and potential areas for innovation.

2.2. TRIZ (Theory of Inventive Problem Solving):
- TRIZ is a systematic innovation methodology that helps individuals identify inventive solutions by leveraging principles and patterns observed in inventive patents.
- Explanation: TRIZ offers a structured approach to problem-solving by drawing on a vast database of inventive solutions.

2.3. Six Thinking Hats:
- The Six Thinking Hats method, developed by Edward de Bono, encourages individuals to view a problem from different perspectives, such as creativity, information, emotions, and more.
- Explanation: This method ensures a comprehensive examination of a problem, leading to innovative solutions.

2.4. Lean Startup Methodology:

- The Lean Startup methodology advocates for iterative development and testing of ideas. It emphasizes rapid prototyping, customer feedback, and continuous improvement.
- Explanation: This approach minimizes risk by validating ideas early in the development process, leading to more innovative and successful outcomes.

2.5. Open Innovation:

- Open innovation involves collaborating with external partners, such as customers, suppliers, and research institutions, to access a broader pool of ideas and expertise.
- Explanation: Open innovation expands the scope of innovation by tapping into external sources of creativity and knowledge.

Section 3: Real-World Examples of Innovative Thinkers

Innovative thinkers often serve as beacons of inspiration, demonstrating the power of creative problem-solving and innovation. Let's draw insight from real-world examples:

3.1. Elon Musk:

- Elon Musk, the visionary entrepreneur behind companies like SpaceX and Tesla, exemplifies innovative thinking. His ventures push the boundaries of space exploration and sustainable energy solutions.
- Explanation: Musk's determination to colonize Mars and revolutionize the automotive industry demonstrates the potential of innovative thinking to reshape entire industries.

3.2. Thomas Edison:

- Thomas Edison, the prolific inventor, held over 1,000 patents and played a pivotal role in the development of the electric light bulb, the phonograph, and many other innovations.
- Explanation: Edison's relentless experimentation and problem-solving techniques continue to inspire inventors and innovators.

3.3. Steve Jobs:

- Steve Jobs, the co-founder of Apple Inc., was known for his visionary approach to product design and user experience. He transformed industries with groundbreaking products like the iPhone and iPad.
- Explanation: Jobs' emphasis on design, simplicity, and user-centric innovation set a benchmark for the technology industry.

3.4. Marie Curie:

- Marie Curie, a pioneering physicist and chemist, made groundbreaking discoveries in radioactivity and won Nobel Prizes in both physics and chemistry.
- Explanation: Curie's relentless pursuit of scientific knowledge and innovative research methods revolutionized our understanding of the atom.

3.5. Jeff Bezos:

- Jeff Bezos, the founder of Amazon, transformed the way we shop and consume media. His innovative thinking extended to ventures like Amazon Web Services (AWS) and Blue Origin.
- Explanation: Bezos' customer-centric approach and willingness to take calculated risks exemplify the power of innovative thinking in business.

In conclusion, innovation and problem-solving are essential skills that can be nurtured and developed. Encouraging creative problem-solving, utilizing effective tools and methods, and drawing inspiration from innovative thinkers are key components of fostering innovation. These strategies empower individuals and organizations to tackle complex challenges and drive progress in various fields, from technology to science and beyond.

# 17

# Lifelong Learning and Personal Growth

Lifelong learning refers to the process of acquiring knowledge skills and competencies throughout one's life with the aim of personal growth professional development and intellectual stimulation. It emphasizes the notion that learning is not limited to formal education but extends to all aspects of life. Lifelong learning promotes personal growth by expanding one's horizons enhancing capabilities and fostering adaptability in a rapidly changing world.

In today's fast-paced and knowledge-based society the importance of continuous learning cannot be overstated. Here are some key reasons why lifelong learning and personal growth are crucial:

1. Professional Development: Continuous learning is essential to stay relevant and competitive in the job market. Technology and industries evolve rapidly and acquiring new skills and knowledge keeps professionals ahead of the curve. Lifelong learning allows individuals to enhance their existing skills explore new

areas of interest and adapt to changing job requirements.

2. Personal Growth: Lifelong learning provides opportunities for personal growth and self-improvement. It broadens one's understanding of the world enhances critical thinking and problem-solving abilities and nurtures creativity. Learning new things fosters personal satisfaction and a sense of achievement leading to increased self-confidence and a positive mindset.

3. Cognitive Benefits: Engaging in lifelong learning helps keep the mind sharp and active. It improves memory concentration and cognitive abilities reducing the risk of cognitive decline and age-related diseases such as dementia. Learning new skills and knowledge stimulates the brain and promotes neuroplasticity the brain's ability to form new neural connections.

Now let's explore some strategies for acquiring new skills and knowledge:

1. Formal Education: Pursuing traditional educational programs such as attending universities or colleges is one way to acquire formal qualifications and specialized knowledge.

2. Online Learning: The advent of technology has revolutionized learning making it more accessible and flexible. Online platforms such as e-learning websites massive open online courses (MOOCs and educational video tutorials offer a vast array of subjects and courses to choose from allowing self-paced learning from anywhere at any time.

3. Professional Development Programs: Many organizations

offer professional development programs and workshops to enhance employees' skills and knowledge. These programs often focus on specific job-related skills and provide hands-on training.

4. Networking and Mentoring: Engaging with professionals in your field through networking events and mentorship programs can provide valuable insights and guidance. Mentors can offer advice share experiences and help navigate through challenges.

5. Reading and Self-Study: Reading books articles and research papers in areas of interest can be an excellent way to acquire new knowledge and expand understanding. Self-study allows individuals to explore topics independently and at their own pace.

6. Volunteering and Community Engagement: Participating in community initiatives volunteering and attending workshops and seminars help individuals gain practical skills expand their networks and contribute to society while learning from others.

In addition to these strategies there are various resources and opportunities available for lifelong learning:

1. Libraries: Public and academic libraries offer a wide range of books research materials and resources. They often provide access to databases e-books and online journals to support self-directed learning.

2. Professional Associations: Joining professional organizations or associations relevant to your field provides access to valuable

resources such as conferences webinars and industry-specific publications. These platforms allow individuals to learn from industry leaders and stay updated on current trends.

3. Continuing Education: Many universities and colleges offer continuing education programs specifically tailored for working professionals. These programs often provide specialized knowledge certifications and credentials in a shorter duration than traditional degree programs.

4. Online Communities and Forums: Engaging with online communities and forums related to your areas of interest or profession can foster knowledge-sharing discussions and collaborative learning.

5. Podcasts and Webinars: Podcasts and webinars are a convenient way to access expert insights interviews and discussions on various subject matters. They can be accessed on-demand allowing for personalized learning experiences.

Lifelong learning and personal growth are integral to adapting to a rapidly evolving world expanding one's potential and maintaining a fulfilling and meaningful life. By embracing a continuous learning mindset individuals can unlock new opportunities enhance their skills and thrive in both their personal and professional lives.

# 18

# Ethics and Values

Ethics and values form the moral compass that guides individuals and societies in making choices and conducting themselves. In this comprehensive exploration, we will delve deeply into the role of ethics and values in decision-making, the importance of exploring and aligning with your personal values, and how to navigate ethical dilemmas and find resolutions.

Section 1: The Role of Ethics and Values in Decision-Making

Ethics and values play a fundamental role in shaping the decisions people make in their personal and professional lives. Understanding this role is crucial for making principled and morally sound choices.

1.1. Defining Ethics:

- Ethics refers to the study of what is morally right and wrong. It provides a framework for evaluating actions and decisions based on principles of fairness, justice, and integrity.

- Explanation: Ethics offers a structured approach to evaluating the moral implications of decisions, ensuring they align with societal norms and values.

1.2. Guiding Decision-Making:

- Ethics and values serve as guides for decision-making. They help individuals determine the ethicality of their choices and actions.
- Explanation: When faced with a decision, individuals often consider whether the choice aligns with their values and adheres to ethical principles.

1.3. Business Ethics:

- In the corporate world, business ethics are essential for maintaining trust and reputation. They involve making morally responsible decisions in business practices.
- Explanation: Ethical business practices contribute to long-term success by building trust with customers, employees, and stakeholders.

1.4. Ethical Leadership:

- Ethical leadership involves setting an example by making decisions that prioritize ethical considerations, transparency, and fairness.
- Explanation: Ethical leaders inspire trust and create a culture of integrity within organizations, fostering positive ethical behavior.

Section 2: Exploring Your Personal Values and Aligning Them with Your Actions

Understanding your personal values and ensuring they align with your actions is essential for living an authentic and purposeful life.

2.1. Identifying Personal Values:

- Personal values are deeply held beliefs and principles that guide behavior and decision-making. Identifying these values is a critical step in ethical living.
- Explanation: Self-awareness of personal values helps individuals make decisions that are in harmony with their core beliefs.

2.2. Integrity and Authenticity:

- Living in alignment with your values fosters integrity and authenticity. It means your actions are a true reflection of your beliefs.
- Explanation: Acting in accordance with your values enhances self-respect, credibility, and a sense of purpose.

2.3. Ethical Decision-Making Frameworks:

- Various ethical decision-making frameworks, such as the virtue ethics approach or the utilitarian approach, can help individuals evaluate complex moral dilemmas.
- Explanation: These frameworks offer structured methods for assessing ethical dilemmas and reaching principled decisions.

2.4. Ethical Codes of Conduct:

- Many professions and organizations have established ethical codes of conduct. Adhering to these codes is essential for ethical behavior in specific contexts.

- Explanation: Ethical codes provide clear guidelines for professionals, ensuring their actions align with industry-specific ethical standards.

## Section 3: Ethical Dilemmas and Their Resolutions

Ethical dilemmas are situations in which individuals must make difficult choices between conflicting moral principles. Navigating these dilemmas requires ethical reasoning and careful consideration.

3.1. Types of Ethical Dilemmas:

- Ethical dilemmas can manifest in various forms, including conflicts between personal and professional values, competing ethical principles, or moral obligations.
- Explanation: Recognizing the different types of ethical dilemmas is the first step in addressing them effectively.

3.2. Ethical Decision-Making Process:

- Ethical decision-making involves assessing the situation, considering ethical principles, exploring potential consequences, and arriving at a principled resolution.
- Explanation: Following a systematic process ensures that ethical dilemmas are approached with thoughtfulness and integrity.

3.3. Balancing Conflicting Values:

- Some ethical dilemmas involve balancing conflicting values or principles. Finding a resolution may require compromise or creative solutions.
- Explanation: Balancing conflicting values is a challenging

aspect of ethical decision-making that calls for careful deliberation.

3.4. Seeking Guidance and Counsel:

- In complex ethical dilemmas, seeking guidance from trusted mentors, colleagues, or ethics committees can provide valuable perspectives and insights.
- Explanation: Consulting others can help individuals gain a more comprehensive understanding of ethical dilemmas and potential solutions.

3.5. Ethical Leadership in Resolutions:

- Ethical leaders play a vital role in facilitating ethical dilemma resolutions within organizations. They set a tone of ethical behavior and provide guidance in challenging situations.
- Explanation: Ethical leadership fosters a culture where ethical dilemmas are addressed openly and resolved in alignment with shared values.

Real-World Examples of Ethics and Values:

1. Whistleblower Edward Snowden: Snowden's decision to expose classified government surveillance programs reflected his belief in the importance of transparency, accountability, and personal values over loyalty to an organization.

2. Philanthropist Melinda Gates: Melinda Gates' commitment to philanthropy and addressing global health and equity issues exemplifies her values-driven approach to making a positive impact on the world.

3. Humanitarian Dr. Paul Farmer: Dr. Paul Farmer's work in global health, particularly in providing medical care to underserved populations, reflects his deep commitment to social justice and the value of every human life.

4. Journalist and Activist Malala Yousafzai: Malala's advocacy for girls' education and women's rights, despite facing threats and violence, demonstrates her unwavering commitment to her values and the principles of equality and education for all.

In conclusion, ethics and values serve as moral guides for decision-making, ensuring that actions align with personal principles and societal standards. Exploring personal values, living authentically, and navigating ethical dilemmas with integrity are integral to leading a principled and purposeful life. Real-world examples of individuals who have upheld their values in challenging circumstances inspire others to prioritize ethics and values in their own lives.

# 19

# Environmental and Social Responsibility

Environmental awareness and sustainability are crucial in today's world to address the challenges of climate change resource depletion and environmental degradation. It involves understanding the impact of human activities on the planet and taking actions to minimize negative consequences while promoting positive change. Let's delve deeper into the significance of environmental awareness and sustainability:

1. Environmental Awareness:

Environmental awareness involves recognizing and understanding the interconnectedness between humans and the environment. It includes knowledge about key environmental issues such as climate change pollution habitat destruction and loss of biodiversity. By raising awareness individuals communities and businesses can make informed decisions to mitigate their environmental impact.

Environmental awareness helps society recognize the urgent need for action and encourages conservation efforts. It prompts individuals and organizations to adopt environmentally-friendly practices and make sustainable choices in their daily lives or operations.

2. Sustainability:

Sustainability is the idea of meeting the needs of the present without compromising the ability of future generations to meet their own needs. It considers the social economic and environmental aspects of human activities to ensure long-term well-being for both current and future generations. Three pillars of sustainability include:

- Environmental Sustainability: This focuses on minimizing resource consumption reducing pollution and waste conserving natural resources and preserving ecosystems. Sustainable practices aim to restore and maintain the health of the planet.

- Social Sustainability: This emphasizes creating equitable and inclusive communities where everyone's well-being is prioritized. It involves promoting social justice human rights fair economic opportunities and access to education healthcare and basic necessities.

- Economic Sustainability: This entails ensuring long-term economic viability while minimizing negative impacts. It involves sustainable business practices responsible investment decisions and fostering a circular economy to reduce waste and promote resource efficiency.

Engaging in social responsibility and community involvement:

Social responsibility refers to the ethical obligation of individuals organizations and governments to act in ways that benefit society as a whole. It involves addressing social and environmental issues and making positive contributions to communities. Community involvement is an integral component of social responsibility as it fosters a sense of togetherness and a shared commitment to social well-being.

Engaging in social responsibility can take various forms such as:

1. Philanthropy: Supporting non-profit organizations and causes through financial contributions or in-kind donations.

2. Volunteerism: Offering time expertise and skills to support community initiatives and projects such as cleaning campaigns charity events or mentorship programs.

3. Corporate Social Responsibility (CSR): Companies can integrate social and environmental concerns into their business operations supply chains and stakeholder interactions. This may include initiatives like employee volunteering sustainable sourcing or investing in renewable energy.

By actively participating in social responsibility and community involvement individuals and organizations can positively impact society address social issues and contribute to the overall well-being of communities.

Sustainable living practices:

Sustainable living refers to adopting lifestyle choices and practices that minimize negative environmental impacts and promote a more sustainable future. It involves being mindful of resource consumption waste generation and the overall ecological footprint. Some sustainable living practices include:

1. Energy Efficiency: Reducing energy consumption by using energy-efficient appliances optimizing insulation in buildings and utilizing renewable energy sources like solar or wind.

2. Waste Reduction and Recycling: Implementing practices to reduce waste recycling materials and composting organic waste to minimize landfill contributions.

3. Sustainable Transportation: Choosing public transportation walking cycling or using electric vehicles instead of relying heavily on private cars which contribute to air pollution and greenhouse gas emissions.

4. Responsible Consumption: Making conscious choices about the products we buy considering their environmental impact supporting local and sustainable businesses and reducing unnecessary consumption.

5. Water Conservation: Conserving water through practices like efficient irrigation graywater recycling and minimizing water wastage in households.

By adopting sustainable living practices individuals can minimize their ecological footprint contribute to a healthier environment and inspire others to make sustainable choices.

In summary deepening environmental awareness and embracing sustainability are vital in addressing environmental challenges and shaping a better future. Engaging in social responsibility and community involvement further reinforces these efforts fostering collective responsibility towards a more equitable and sustainable society. Sustainable living practices empower individuals to reduce their environmental impact and inspire others to follow suit. Together these actions contribute to a more environmentally and socially responsible world.

# 20

# Setting and Achieving Stretch Goals

Setting and achieving stretch goals involves pushing the boundaries of what is considered achievable. In this comprehensive exploration, we will dive deeply into the concept of stretch goals, strategies for setting and pursuing ambitious, long-term objectives, and how to overcome obstacles and maintain commitment when striving for challenging targets.

Section 1: Going Beyond SMART Goals

While SMART (Specific, Measurable, Achievable, Relevant, Time-bound) goals provide a structured framework for setting objectives, stretch goals require a different approach, as they often involve aiming for what may seem unattainable.

1.1. Defining Stretch Goals:

- Stretch goals are ambitious, long-term targets that go beyond the scope of traditional SMART goals. They challenge individuals or organizations to achieve extraordinary results.
- Explanation: Stretch goals inspire innovation, creativity,

and a commitment to continuous improvement by pushing individuals out of their comfort zones.

1.2. Stretch vs. SMART Goals:

- Contrasting stretch goals with SMART goals highlights the key differences, such as the level of ambition, time frame, and degree of challenge.
- Explanation: SMART goals are typically achievable within existing capabilities, while stretch goals require significant growth and development.

1.3. Psychological Impact:

- Setting stretch goals can have a profound psychological impact, motivating individuals to aim higher and reach their full potential.
- Explanation: Stretch goals encourage a growth mindset, as individuals believe they can expand their abilities and achieve more than they initially thought possible.

1.4. Risk and Reward:

- Stretch goals often come with higher risks, as failure is a possibility. However, the rewards of accomplishing such goals can be substantial in terms of personal growth and organizational success.
- Explanation: Risk-taking is inherent in setting stretch goals, but calculated risks can lead to exceptional achievements.

Section 2: Strategies for Setting and Pursuing Ambitious, Long-Term Goals

Achieving stretch goals requires a strategic approach that involves careful planning, persistence, and adaptability.

2.1. Vision and Clarity:

- Clearly defining the desired outcome and having a compelling vision are crucial for setting and pursuing stretch goals.

- Explanation: A well-defined vision serves as a guiding star, inspiring commitment and focus.

2.2. Breakdown and Milestones:

- Breaking down a stretch goal into smaller, manageable milestones makes the path to success more achievable and less overwhelming.

- Explanation: Milestones create a sense of progress and provide opportunities for celebration along the journey.

2.3. Continuous Learning and Adaptation:

- Embracing a learning mindset allows individuals and organizations to adapt and make necessary adjustments when pursuing stretch goals.

- Explanation: The ability to learn from failures and setbacks is essential for staying on course and optimizing strategies.

2.4. Resource Allocation:

- Allocating resources strategically, whether they are financial, human, or technological, ensures that the pursuit of stretch goals is well-supported.

- Explanation: Adequate resources are necessary to overcome challenges and seize opportunities.

2.5. Innovation and Creativity:

- Encouraging innovation and creative problem-solving is

integral to achieving stretch goals, as they often require unconventional approaches.

- Explanation: Innovations can lead to breakthroughs that propel progress toward stretch goals.

Section 3: Overcoming Obstacles and Staying Committed

The path to achieving stretch goals is seldom smooth. Overcoming obstacles and maintaining unwavering commitment are key to success.

3.1. Resilience and Perseverance:

- Resilience, the ability to bounce back from setbacks, and perseverance, the determination to keep moving forward, are vital attributes when pursuing stretch goals.
- Explanation: Setbacks are part of the journey, and resilience allows individuals to overcome them without losing sight of the goal.

3.2. Adaptive Leadership:

- Adaptive leadership involves adjusting strategies and approaches based on evolving circumstances and feedback.
- Explanation: Effective leadership is essential for steering the course and keeping the team motivated.

3.3. Collaborative Teams:

- Building a collaborative and supportive team is essential for achieving stretch goals. Team members can offer diverse perspectives and skills.
- Explanation: Collaboration enhances problem-solving and provides a network of support during challenging times.

3.4. Continuous Evaluation:

- Regularly evaluating progress and performance is crucial for staying on track and making necessary adjustments.
- Explanation: Ongoing assessment ensures that strategies remain relevant and effective.

3.5. Celebrating Achievements:

- Celebrating small victories and milestones along the way boosts morale and reinforces commitment to the ultimate stretch goal.
- Explanation: Celebrations provide motivation and a sense of accomplishment, fueling the drive to continue.

Real-World Examples of Stretch Goals:

1. NASA's Moonshot: NASA's Apollo program set an audacious stretch goal of landing humans on the moon. The program involved overcoming numerous technological challenges and uncertainties, ultimately resulting in the historic Apollo 11 moon landing in 1969.

2. Elon Musk's Mars Colonization: Elon Musk's SpaceX aims to colonize Mars, an extraordinarily ambitious long-term goal that requires significant advancements in space travel technology and sustainability.

3. Tesla's Electric Vehicle Revolution: Tesla set out to revolutionize the automotive industry by making electric vehicles mainstream. This stretch goal has not only transformed the automotive sector but also accelerated the global shift toward sustainable transportation.

4. Google's Quantum Supremacy: Google achieved quantum supremacy, a milestone in quantum computing, by demonstrating that its quantum computer could perform a specific task faster than the most advanced classical supercomputer.

5. Bill and Melinda Gates Foundation's Global Health Impact: The Gates Foundation set a stretch goal to significantly reduce global poverty and improve healthcare access worldwide, making a substantial impact on public health and education.

In conclusion, setting and achieving stretch goals involves aspiring to extraordinary accomplishments, even in the face of significant challenges and uncertainties. Strategies for pursuing such goals require a clear vision, careful planning, resilience, and adaptability. Real-world examples demonstrate that stretch goals can drive innovation and transformation on a grand scale, inspiring individuals and organizations to reach for the extraordinary.

9 789391 927820

Printed at Repro India Ltd.